A Publication of the
National Wildfire
Coordinating Group

AGENCY ADMINISTRATOR'S GUIDE TO CRITICAL INCIDENT MANAGEMENT

PMS 926   JULY 2008

Agency Administrator:

Agency Name and Location:

Agency Administrator's Guide to Critical Incident Management

JULY 2008
PMS 926

Sponsored for NWCG publication by the Safety and Health Working Team.
Questions regarding <u>content</u> may be addressed to the NWCG's Executive Secretary at: nwcg_executive_secretary@nifc.blm.gov or agency representatives of the Safety and Health Working Team.

This publication is available for download at http://www.nwcg.gov/pms/pubs/pubs.htm.

Preface

Agency Administrator's Guide to Critical Incident Management was developed by an interagency group of experts with guidance from the Safety and Health Working Team under authority of the National Wildfire Coordinating Group (NWCG).

The NWCG appreciates the efforts of personnel and all those who have contributed to the development of this guide.

Contents

Introduction

The Agency Administrator's Guide to Critical Incident Management is designed to assist Agency Administrators in dealing with critical incidents. A critical incident may be defined as a fatality or other event that can have serious long-term adverse effects on the agency, its employees and their families or the community. Although fire incidents inspired this document, it also has application to other types of incidents.

The Agency Administrator is the highest-ranking agency line officer with direct responsibility for the personnel involved in the incident (for example, BLM District Manager, Park Superintendent, Forest Supervisor, Refuge Manager, BIA Agency Superintendent or State land manager). Through effective, efficient, and timely leadership, Agency Administrators are responsible for the overall management of critical incidents within their jurisdiction.

This document includes a series of checklists to guide an Agency Administrator through those difficult and chaotic days that follow a death, serious injury, or other critical or highly visible event. *The time to use it is now!* This document needs to be reviewed and updated at least annually. The guide has been document protected; however, editing is permissible within the shaded areas.

The availability of Critical Incident Stress Management (CISM) teams and related resources varies constantly – it is imperative that local units pre-identify in this plan the CISM resources that can support local unit needs.

This guide was designed as a working tool to assist Agency Administrators with the chronological steps in managing the incident. It also provides a detailed overview of Agency Administrators' responsibilities before a critical incident occurs, during the actual management of the incident, and after the incident activity has taken place. It is not intended to take the place of local emergency plans or other detailed guidance. It should be used in conjunction with other references as well as the attached appendixes.

This guide can also be used as a worksheet (both in preparation for and in management of a critical incident) by Agency Administrators and others with oversight responsibilities during a critical incident. Every office should ensure that the **BEFORE** actions are initially completed by a specific date and then updated each year. The worksheets may also be used as a guide in conducting practice exercises.

It is recommended that, as part of the **BEFORE** preparation as well as during the management of a critical incident, units insert specific local information into this worksheet (e.g., key contacts, phone numbers, additional steps based on local emergency plan, names of local employees and others who would be assigned specific responsibilities).

Terms that may be unfamiliar to some users are defined in the Glossary (Appendix H).

BEFORE

THE

INCIDENT

#	BEFORE	CONTACTS/ PHONE #S	ASSIGNED TO	STATUS
Agency Administrator Roles and Responsibilities				
1	Determine what types of incidents are likely to occur on lands for which you are responsible. Type: • Fire • Law Enforcement • Aviation • Vehicle Accident • • • • •			
2	Identify those agencies that have statutory/jurisdictional responsibilities for those incidents.			
3	Pre-plan incident response and develop criteria on when and how to implement ICS organizational structure for the critical incident (e.g., not all critical incidents require an ICS organization).			
4	Prepare a Delegation of Authority for the critical incident management team. The delegation can be edited at the time of the incident to reflect specific complexity and scope.			
5	Ensure ALL employees have current emergency notification information on file (secured yet accessible). Update information as seasonals are hired. (See Emergency Notification Information, Appendix A).			
6	Identify family liaison(s) for when serious injuries or fatalities occur. (See Family Liaison, Appendix B).			
7	Develop local emergency operating plan which includes initial response and notification procedures.			
8	Provide training and conduct exercises focusing on interagency cooperation, coordination, and incident management.			
9	Ensure key personnel designated to manage the critical incident are capable, organized, and clearly understand their roles and responsibilities.			

#	BEFORE	CONTACTS/ PHONE #S	ASSIGNED TO	STATUS
Agency Notification and Reporting				
1	Develop contact list for reporting process (See Agency Reporting Log, Appendix C).			
2	Identify your agency's process for reporting and investigating serious injury or deaths including procedures for reporting shelter deployments and entrapments.			
3	For wildland fire fatalities, entrapments and burnovers, notify the National Interagency Coordination Center (208-387-5400) within 24 hours. Use NWCG Form PMS 405-1 found at: http://www.nwcg.gov/pms/forms_otr/ forms_otr.htm – Individual agency follow-up is still required by Agency Administrator.			
4	Ensure notification of Occupational Safety and Health Administration (OSHA) area office within eight hours for: • Death of any employee from work-related incident. • Inpatient hospitalization of three or more employees as a result of a work related incident. (See External Phone Numbers, Appendix D).			
5	Establish process/protocol for notification of next of kin in case of serious injury or death; coordinate with local authorities. See Fatality/Serious Injury Notification Guide (Appendix E).			
Family Liaison				
1	Identify resources that are available to assist the designated family liaison(s) (see Family Liaison, Appendix B): • Grief counselors • Peer supporters • Administrative support			
2	Identify internal policies that may apply when assisting the family. For example: • A work-related death autopsy may be necessary to ensure family death benefit • Determine what death benefits (funeral and burial costs) would be covered by the agency. • Procedures for processing personnel papers • Determine what advice should be given for filing claims			

#	BEFORE	CONTACTS/ PHONE #S	ASSIGNED TO	STATUS
Critical Incident Stress Management (CISM)				
1	Ensure that CISM protocols and resources are identified prior to the occurrence of a critical incident. • Identify local/regional/area CISM resources (e.g., peer support, defusing, debriefing). • Contact CISM resources to discuss activation/capabilities/costs.			
2	Identify Employee Assistance Program (EAP) and its capabilities in: • Grief counseling • Family support • Critical incident stress support			
Information and Communications				
1	Develop critical incident communication procedures as part of a local emergency operating plan. Include: • Agency jurisdictions • Directory of local/regional/national support • Directory of agency experts – Qualified Public Information Officer or equivalent – Some agencies may have designated crisis communication teams – Experienced crisis communicators may be available under contract or through special hiring authorities • Key spokespersons • List of communication tools and resources needed • Process for setting up communication center • Coordination of information dissemination • Coordinate communication process with accident investigation team			
2	Create fact sheets and bio-sketches: • Agency • Community • Generic format for additional fact sheets/bio-sketches • Glossary of terms			
3	Create media contact lists; include phone and fax numbers.			
4	Identify technical expertise to produce maps and graphics (e.g., directions for family visits to fatality site, directions to memorial service).			
5	Ensure Public Information Officers receive appropriate formal training (including trainee assignments) and participate in simulation exercises.			

#	BEFORE	CONTACTS/ PHONE #S	ASSIGNED TO	STATUS
Administration				
1	Create draft Delegation(s) of Authority to manage critical incident.			
2	Create, review, update, and/or renegotiate Memorandums of Understanding (MOUs), Memorandums of Agreement (MOAs), Blanket Purchase Agreements (BPAs), contracts, and other procurement documents that support the management of serious injuries or fatalities. These may include: • Local law enforcement agencies • Medical facilities • Counseling/CISM services • Lodging facilities			
3	Establish a resource list of experts: • Personal claims • Tort claims • Workers' compensation • Death benefits (e.g., Department of Justice's Public Safety Officer's Benefit)			
4	Establish a list of the nearest medical facilities, burn/trauma centers, hours of operation and transport capabilities. (See External Phone Numbers, Appendix D).			
5	Ensure that emergency notification information is periodically reviewed and updated (must have street addresses; no PO boxes) and that this information is easily accessible in an emergency.			
6	Casual hires/ADs/EFFs are agency employees and are the responsibility of the hiring unit. • Refer to NWCG Interagency Incident Business Management Handbook (IIBMH). • Ensure accurate emergency contact information is recorded on all Fire Time Reports (OF-288).			
7	Reference respective agency guides (e.g., employee casualty guide) that contain: • Benefits available for type of employment. • How to file a claim • When the Social Security Administration (SSA) should be contacted			

#	BEFORE	CONTACTS/ PHONE #S	ASSIGNED TO	STATUS
Investigations				
1	Become familiar with laws/regulations pertaining to local/county/state/tribal jurisdictions and their roles/responsibilities for investigating critical incidents.			
2	Review agency/interdepartmental (e.g., DOI and USFS) accident investigation guidelines/procedures found in agency manuals and wildland fire entrapment reporting/investigation procedures. Information on accident investigations may be found at: http://www.nifc.gov/safety/accident_resources.htm			
3	Meet/develop rapport with key local law enforcement administrators (e.g., sheriff, police chief).			
4	Conduct joint training and simulation exercises, where possible, with cooperators.			
5	Participate in local emergency response and/or public safety council meetings on a regular basis.			

DURING

THE

INCIDENT

#	DURING	CONTACTS/ PHONE #S	ASSIGNED TO	STATUS
During (This section builds on the previous *[BEFORE]* section by implementing the previous identified actions).				
Agency Administrator Roles and Responsibilities				
1	Provide for and emphasize the treatment and care of survivors, coworkers, and their families.			
2	Determine the scope of the incident, identify the involved jurisdictions, and implement initial actions.			
3	Determine the capabilities and limitations of your organization and request assistance (e.g., neighboring unit, State or Regional offices, National).			
4	As warranted, provide a Delegation of Authority and objectives for the management of the critical incident.			
5	Determine the level of management required by using pre-identified criteria for implementation of ICS organizational structure (e.g., not all critical incidents require an ICS organization).			
6	Implement reporting/notification procedures, see Agency Reporting Log, Appendix C). Participate personally whenever possible.			
7	Identify key contacts during the critical incident (See Key Contacts During Critical Incident, Appendix F).			
8	When off-unit employees are involved, personally contact Agency Administrator for victim's home duty station with as much information as possible, including names and telephone numbers of contacts.			
9	Prepare for accident investigation. (See Preparing for Serious Accident Investigation Team (SAIT), Appendix G).			
10	Determine need for, and level of, Critical Incident Stress Management (CISM) and implement accordingly. Advise SAIT of CISM actions taken.			
11	Monitor the management of the critical incident. Be readily available to provide direction, guidance and support as needed.			

#	DURING	CONTACTS/ PHONE #S	ASSIGNED TO	STATUS
Initial Action Checklist				
1	Conduct risk assessment on rescue/recovery operations.			
2	Ensure that rescue/recovery response is activated. • For burn injuries ensure that agency protocols are followed.			
3	Gather and verify initial information: **Who:** Full names of victims, including nicknames **When:** Approximate time and date of accident **What:** Suspected cause of injury, death, etc. **Where:** Location of accident (incident name, closest town, jurisdiction, or other geographic information)			
4	Implement local emergency operating plan and critical incident communication procedures. • Ensure that communications are controlled to guarantee privacy of names until next of kin are notified. – Instruct incident personnel not to use communication methods that could compromise privacy and not to use names of victims if communications can be monitored.			
5	**For agency employees from your unit:** • Obtain victims' personal emergency notification information and make notification to next of kin. (See Fatality/Serious Injury Notification Guide, Appendix E). **For off-unit or other agency employees:** • Communicate with off-unit victims' home duty stations until his/her liaison arrives to coordinate with the on-scene agency.			
6	In case of serious injury or death to a Native American, immediately contact the home tribal leadership for cultural considerations.			

#	DURING	CONTACTS/ PHONE #S	ASSIGNED TO	STATUS
Agency Notification and Reporting				
1	Implement agency notification procedures. (See Agency Reporting Log, Appendix C).			
2	Prior to official notification to next of kin, do not release victims' names. (See Fatality/Serious Injury Notification Guide, Appendix E).			
3	Coordinate with law enforcement, coroner or medical examiner. (See Preparing for Serious Accident Investigation Team (SAIT), Appendix G).			
4	Immediately notify critical incident Public Information Officer when family and other internal notification is complete so public release of information may proceed in a timely manner (refer to page 14). • Initial agency press release will be made by the designated Public Information Officer to preserve integrity of notification process. • Recognize that impacts to local communities and others may be significant, depending on the nature of the incident. • State only facts; DO NOT SPECULATE! • Keep employees (including injured survivors) informed about details of the incident as well as schedule of events to follow.			
Family Liaison				
1	Designate family liaison(s). (Refer to Family Liaison, Appendix B). • Consideration should be given to unique circumstances (e.g., non-traditional family situations) and need for multiple family liaisons. • Assign one person per family, but consider the need for other individuals to assist. • Allow the designated family liaison the opportunity to decline the assignment.			
2	Coordinate communication among liaisons.			
3	The family liaison should be available to the family within the first 24 hours. • Consider need for appropriate representative(s) at locations where family members may be present (e.g., hospitals, helicopter/ambulance shuttle points) to assist with their needs.			

#	DURING	CONTACTS/ PHONE #S	ASSIGNED TO	STATUS
4	Facilitate family attendance at agency sponsored events (e.g., memorials).			
5	Consider facilitating networking between families, survivors, and coworkers.			
6	Provide family members access to the Employee Assistance Program (EAP).			
Critical Incident Stress Management (CISM)				
1	As needed, activate CISM resources.			
2	For critical incidents that occur during incidents managed by an Incident Management Team (IMT), the Human Resource Specialist (HRSP), if assigned, may be able to assist the local unit with identifying CISM needs.			
3	Coordinate CISM logistics: • Location away from incident and media • Transportation • Refreshments • Lodging			
4	Ensure that CISM resources can handle the magnitude of debriefing requirements. • Identify approximate number of employees that have a need for CISM services. • Contact CISM resources and discuss approximate numbers of participating employees, timeframes for mobilization and conducting CISM sessions, and participant limits per session.			
5	CISM is generally implemented within 48-72 hours of the critical event. Consideration the following: • Initial CISM provided to personnel directly involved in the incident (e.g., survivors, rescue workers, Incident Management Team members, dispatchers). • Relieving involved personnel from external responsibilities. • Keep crews together, if possible. • Hold separate sessions for personnel involved in the immediate critical incident and outside peers/coworkers.			
6	Ensure confidentiality throughout the CISM process.			

#	DURING	CONTACTS/ PHONE #S	ASSIGNED TO	STATUS
Information and Communications				
1	Implement critical incident communication procedures. Needs may vary based on complexity of the critical incident. • Develop communication strategy. • Set up communication center facilities. • Publicize information hotline telephone number and location. • Consider establishing an "800" phone number to facilitate information flow. • Consider establishing a website to provide current critical incident information. • Use internal bulletin boards to communicate with employees.			
2	Place order(s) for qualified incident information officer(s) or equivalent. • Designate a lead Public Information Officer.			
3	Confirm roles and responsibilities, and ensure that appropriate coordination occurs. • Local unit Public Information Officer • Incident Management Team Public Information Officer (if IMT is assigned) • Cooperator Information Officer(s) • Incoming critical incident information resources • Serious Accident Investigation Team's Information Officer(s)			
4	Establish approval process for release of information. • Designate primary spokesperson for external release of information. • Provide information to victim/family first. – Respond quickly and compassionately. • Names of fatality victims can be released as soon as next of kin have been notified. • Never release names of injured or missing victims.			
5	Brief receptionists, dispatchers, and others on routing/handling of incoming calls and visitors. • Provide Public Information Officer assistance at dispatch centers and reception areas, if appropriate.			
6	Make immediate contact with local media and develop positive relationships with them.			

#	DURING	CONTACTS/ PHONE #S	ASSIGNED TO	STATUS
7	Be prepared to respond to media inquiries within minutes. Use the media to deliver important messages to the public. • Develop an initial prepared statement. • Show concern. • Say what is being done and how quickly the agency responded. • Tell what resources responded. • Give any verified, releasable facts that are available. • Report current status. • Do not speculate or talk off the record; STATE ONLY FACTS. • Confirm the obvious. • Discuss initiation of investigation/review, if appropriate. • Stress that safety of rescue crews, Serious Accident Investigation Team, community, and others is paramount. • Mention environmental impacts, if appropriate. • Thank cooperators. • Inform the public what they can do to help.			
8	Ensure appropriate communications with (may require designated leads): • Internal – within local unit • Interagency – agency cooperators • External – general public, media, public officials			
9	Document all events, contacts, etc. • Chronology • Contact Log • Photos			
10	Have maps and graphics available.			
11	Use media to get messages to the public. Develop an initial prepared statement. • Need for volunteers, along with contact point, if appropriate • Safety messages • Need for cooperation, road closures, etc. • Fire restrictions • Wildland/urban interface issues			
12	Ensure technical experts (e.g., safety, aviation, fire behavior) are available and prepared for media interviews.			

#	DURING	CONTACTS/ PHONE #S	ASSIGNED TO	STATUS
13	Provide and coordinate media access to incident site in cooperation with the Incident Management Team and Serious Accident Investigation Team. • Brief media on incident site and air restrictions. • Consider media pool arrangements.			
14	Anticipate media's needs. • Logistical (e.g., phones, work areas) • Photos/biography(s) of victim(s) • Deadlines • Protective gear • Photo and video opportunities • Interviews			
15	Take advantage of existing newsletters and other established communication tools.			
16	Keep the community and affected landowners/users informed and involved; establish a community liaison position, as necessary.			
17	Provide Public Information Officer support through family liaison, for victims, families, and survivors; local/distant/hospitals.			
18	Protect the rights of those employees who do not want media contact.			
19	Coordinate media access at funerals, memorial services, etc., with family liaison(s).			
20	Prepare agency condolence letters within 24 hours, if possible. Coordinate at all levels within the agency.			
21	Prepare for official visits (e.g., top agency management, governor, mayor, members of congress). • Briefing material, facts/statistics about area, talking point, or speeches, if appropriate. • Assign liaisons/escorts. • Arrange for transportation. • Schedule and facilitate press conference(s), if desired. • Provide mechanism for keeping them involved/informed.			

#	**DURING**	**CONTACTS/ PHONE #S**	**ASSIGNED TO**	**STATUS**
Administration				
1	Develop additional Delegation(s) of Authority, MOUs, MOAs, BPAs and other agreements as required.			
2	Evaluate local unit's added workload and request assistance as needed. • Request help from people (coaches) who have experience in this type of incident. • Request additional personnel to maintain daily operations. • Consider requesting relief from identified work targets for affected personnel.			
3	Designate individual(s) to take lead in preparing/processing required paperwork. • Worker's compensation • Death benefits (Provide a benefits package to families so they are aware of all entitlements.) • Department of Justice's Public Safety Officer's Benefit			
4	Designate a records person familiar with documentation needs and Freedom of Information Act (FOIA) regulations.			
5	Designate a single source for administrative record keeping and tracking throughout the critical incident.			
6	Designate individual(s) to coordinate and be responsible for securing, gathering, and returning personal items, including vehicles and items from lockers or desks.			
7	Identify a fiscal representative to give advice on administrative questions associated with: • Paying travel costs of family members • Transportation costs for the deceased • Funerals and memorials • Other funding questions that may arise			
8	Assist Serious Accident Investigation Team as needed.			

#	DURING	CONTACTS/ PHONE #S	ASSIGNED TO	STATUS
Investigations				
1	Ensure the investigation team(s) receives a thorough briefing about: • What happened – Review initial report. • Jurisdictions involved • Current activities. – Search and rescue – Other investigations • Lists of personnel involved (injuries, fatalities, etc.) – Status – Location – How to contact – Agency • Key officials • Cooperators • Safety Officers • Criminal/civil implications			
2	If a fatality or serious injuries have occurred, a Serious Accident Investigation Team will likely be appointed by a higher-level. The local Agency Administrator should be prepared to host and cooperate with the Serious Accident Investigation Team. (See Preparing for Serious Accident Investigation Team (SAIT), Appendix G).			
3	Clarify and agree upon roles, responsibilities, authorities, and objectives. • Determine who provides Delegation(s) of Authority (at what level of organization). • Determine how public information will be handled and designate a spokesperson (refer to the Information and Communications section on page 14).			
4	Coordinate with Serious Accident Investigation Team in forwarding pertinent safety information through agency channels (e.g., preliminary reports, safety alerts).			
5	Make local unit agency law enforcement available to serve as a liaison between the investigation team(s) and local law enforcement entities.			

AFTER

THE

INCIDENT

#	AFTER	CONTACTS/ PHONE #S	ASSIGNED TO	STATUS
Agency Administrator Roles and Responsibilities				
1	Ensure that key individuals (families, survivors and other appropriate individuals) are briefed on the accident investigation report prior to its release.			
2	When accident investigation reports are released, make subject-matter experts available to answer families' questions and concerns.			
3	Debrief and release CISM providers.			
4	Monitor stress reactions and cumulative stress in agency employees, especially during: • Release of investigative reports and incident management review reports • Anniversary dates • Memorial services Provide Employee Assistance Program (EAP) and other sources for assistance.			
5	Ensure that administrative requirements for affected employees and families (e.g., compensation for claims, benefits) are expedited.			
6	Conduct an After Action Review (AAR) of the management of the critical incident. Develop recommendations for improvement and incorporate into existing plans and share lessons learned. • Address how well agency worked with local, state, and federal cooperators. • Determine if the local emergency plan was effective. • Identify weak areas. • Update this plan as necessary.			
7	Follow up on recommendations/corrective actions from accident investigation reports.			

#	AFTER	CONTACTS/ PHONE #S	ASSIGNED TO	STATUS
Family Liaison				
1	Continue working with family members concerning: • Claims and benefits • Information requests (e.g., media interviews) • Visiting site of incident • Assistance with writing obituary as requested • Funeral arrangements			
2	Ensure that family liaison(s) receive debriefing/stress counseling as necessary.			
3	Continue to communicate regularly with families, but establish a mutually agreed-upon conclusion to official involvement.			
4	Provide family with information on follow-up resources (e.g., Wildland Firefighter Foundation).			
5	Brief family on the potential of future contacts (e.g., media attention during anniversaries).			
Information and Communications				
1	Develop a communication transition plan to ensure the dissemination of information regarding the critical incident. • Address continuing impacts, staff rides, visitors, traffic, media, production companies, etc. • Identify potential need for follow-up committee. • Potential requests for dedication memorials (plaques and statues). • Plan for facilitating return visits to the incident site by family members/ survivors/visitors. • Evaluate public information activities; adjust communication plan as appropriate. • Develop mechanism for dissemination for follow-up information to family members/survivors.			
2	Prepare thank-you letters and commendations.			
3	Complete any pending documentation.			

#	AFTER	CONTACTS/ PHONE #S	ASSIGNED TO	STATUS
Administration				
1	Follow up with designated Freedom of Information Act (FOIA) contact person for the archiving and dissemination of information.			
2	Assist survivors and family members with paperwork as necessary. <ul><li>Worker's compensation benefits.</li><li>Death benefits</li><li>Other benefits as applicable</li></ul>			
3	If requested, provide the process for filing tort claims.			
4	Obtain contact information for fiscal and contracting experts who were assigned during the critical incident.			
Investigations				
1	Ensure accident investigation team closes out with: <ul><li>Agency Administrator</li><li>Agency officials at appropriate levels</li></ul>			

EMERGENCY NOTIFICATION INFORMATION
Appendix A

	Date Prepared	
Last Name	First Name	Middle Initial

Physical Address		

City	State	Zip Code

Home Phone	Date of Birth	Social Security Number

PRIMARY NEXT OF KIN NOTIFICATION

Last Name	First Name	Relationship

Physical Home Address (No PO Box)

City	State

Primary Phone Number	Secondary Phone Number
Primary Next of Kin's Place of Work	Phone Number at Work

Primary Next of Kin's Physical Work Address

City	State

Any known medical conditions to be advised of when making any notification to the primary next of kin? (List)

Who would you like to make notification of major injury or death to your primary next of kin?	Phone number to reach this person

CHILDREN

Last Name	First Name	Phone Number	Date of Birth
Physical Address			
City	State		
Last Name	First Name	Phone Number	Date of Birth
Physical Address			
City	State		

SECONDARY NEXT OF KIN NOTIFICATION

Please indicate a second next of kin whom you would want to be notified if the primary next of kin is not available.

Last Name	First Name	Relationship

Physical Address (No PO Box)

City	State

Primary Phone Number	Secondary Phone Number
Secondary Next of Kin's Place of Work	Phone Number at Work

Secondary Next of Kin's Physical Work Address

City	State

Any known medical conditions to be advised of when making any notification to the secondary next of kin? (List)

Who would you like to make notification of major injury or death to your secondary next of kin?	Phone number to reach this person

MEDICAL

In the event of a major injury and you are unconscious, what are your wishes regarding life support services?

Who has rights to carry out your wishes regarding life support services?

What are your wishes regarding blood transfusions?	What is your blood type?

Are you an organ donor?

Name of clergy, priest, or minister to be notified *(Optional)*

Denomination *(Optional)*

Are there any people you would **not** like notified in case of major injury or death?

Are there any pets that need immediate care? If so, where are they located?

FAMILY LIAISON
Appendix B

The family liaison is critical in facilitating communication between the agency and the family. The family liaison must be capable of ensuring that agency needs are met while providing assistance to families. This balancing act occurs in an emotionally charged atmosphere that can be stressful to the liaison. Agencies should be mindful of selecting the appropriate person to act as family liaison. Select one family liaison per family but consider the need for other individuals to assist.

Considerations for Selecting Family Liaison(s):

- Try to have local liaisons, if possible.

- The family liaison should be available to the family within the first 24 hours.

- Being a family liaison is a long-term commitment that will often impact work. Family liaisons can work with families for years.

- Give consideration to identifying a pair of employees to serve as family liaisons. This will provide a backup contact and allow family liaisons to brief each other.

- Carefully weigh the pros (immediate rapport/trust) and cons (emotional involvement lack of objectivity) of assigning a family liaison who is a friend of the family.

- Select a steady, level-headed individual who is a good listener and communicator and will likely maintain their objectivity.

- A family liaison must be willing to take on the job, with an understanding of the emotional and time demands involved. Allow the selected liaison the opportunity to decline the assignment.

Preparations for the Family Liaison

- Prepare yourself physically, mentally and emotionally before visiting the family.

- Wearing a uniform or professional attire may be appropriate for the initial visit.

- Have another person accompany you on your first visit; establish his/her role.

- Anticipate questions and be prepared. Keep an ongoing record of activities so you can remember to follow up on all requests.

- Do not assume you know what the families and survivors want…ASK. Do not burden the family with unnecessary requests or demands. Try to ask 'yes' or 'no' questions when decisions are required.

- Be prepared to meet the family at other locations, such as hospitals, helicopter/ambulance shuttle points and other public areas.

- Coordinate with other family liaisons in the event of multiple fatalities or serious injuries. Consider scheduling daily conference calls or meetings.

Communicating With Families

This section is a summary of key principles that are useful for communicating effectively with next of kin and other family members.

The first principles are for responding to emotion. Strong emotional responses by the next of kin can be expected and may be very helpful to long-term acceptance and readjustment.

Important points are LISTEN and DO NOT ARGUE. "Listening" is different from "hearing"— people hear with their ears, but listen with their minds. No matter what the family says, do not argue. It will not help and usually makes the situation worse.

Negative information and high-stress situations tend to make people defensive. Almost any information can be presented either negatively or positively.

Telling people what to do and starting sentences with the word "you" are common triggers for defensiveness. Defensiveness can also be reduced by avoiding general statements and dealing instead with specific needs.

The key factor to giving complicated information is breaking it into small pieces. Do not assume that the information has registered or has been understood. The guideline in this section can save a lot of misunderstanding and future problems.

Assist the family in establishing achievable goals. Some examples may be arrangements for funerals, memorials, meeting with benefits coordinator, etc. Goal-setting is a valuable tool for avoiding problems and keeping communication open. A long-term family representative assignment can lead to over dependence on the part of the next of kin and a dread of letting go of a relationship. Goal setting helps to keep the process focused on the end point of the assignment. A final meeting to officially end the assignment is usually helpful for both the family representative and the next of kin.

Follow-up Contacts

The family liaison should encourage the next of kin to begin funeral arrangements, with consideration given to the return of the remains, desires of the family, when travel arrangements can be made for family members, and agency logistics.

The family liaison in coordination with human resource specialists may need to help the family complete the forms and processing for:

- Office of Workers' Compensation Programs (OWCP)
- Social Security Administration
- Veteran's Administration (if applicable)
- Public Safety Officers Benefit Program (if applicable)
- Agency benefit claims (e.g., 401K, life insurance)

Stay in touch with family. Many times family and friends will care for the immediate needs of the bereaved well, but after a few days this support often disappears especially days after services are held. Would-be supporters might feel that a grieving person would rather face their loss alone. This is the time when the family liaison and supporters are needed the most and must stay in touch more than ever before. Provide families with access to support programs and resources such as Employee Assistance Program (EAP), Wildland Firefighter Foundation, and encourage networking with other affected families and coworkers.

AGENCY REPORTING LOG
Appendix C

Incident: Location:

Employee's Name: Incident Date:

Description of Accident Situation:

Required	Office/Official	Phone Numbers	Completion Date
☐	Agency Director		
☐	Appropriate Agency Administrators		
☐	National Interagency Coordination Center	208-387-5400	
☐	Safety Manager		
☐	Servicing Personnel Officer		
☐	Public Affairs Officer		
☐	Fire Management Officer		
☐	Law Enforcement Staff		
☐	Aviation Management		
☐	Office of Inspector General (if waste, fraud or abuse is indicated)		
☐	Regional/Field Solicitor or Office of the General Counsel		
☐	Tort Claims Officer		
☐	Others:		
☐			
☐			

Task	Remarks	Time/Date Completed

For wildland fire fatalities, entrapments and burnovers, notify the National Interagency Coordination Center (208-387-5400) within 24 hours. Use NWCG Form PMS 405-1.

EXTERNAL PHONE NUMBERS
Appendix D

Organization	Contact Name	Phone Number
OSHA Office		
Police		
Sheriff		
Coroner/Morgue		
Hospital(s)/Clinic(s)	1. 2.	
Burn Centers		
Trauma Units		
Chief-to-Chief Network (NFFF) www.firehero.org/		301-447-1365
Wildland Firefighter Foundation www.wffoundation.org		208-336-2996
Chaplain		
CISM Resources		
Employee Assistance Program (EAP)		

FATALITY/SERIOUS INJURY NOTIFICATION GUIDE
Appendix E

The following information will provide some guidelines for preparing and completing fatality/serious injury notifications. The notification process needs to be done quickly and with the utmost sensitivity when an employee fatality or serious injury occurs. As the agency representative you are expected to be sensitive, courteous, sympathetic and helpful toward the next of kin during the notification. Your presence is designed to demonstrate that the agency is genuinely concerned with its personnel and their families.

Each notification is unique as a result of the individuals and circumstances surrounding the death or serious injury, and will garner different reactions. Your alertness to the needs of the family will assist in maintaining a rapport with next of kin at the time of their greatest need. Your personal action and words in this sensitive task will reflect on the agency's image as well as instill confidence in the agency with the survivors. Line Officers are usually responsible to make the notification; however, other personnel may be called to assist in this task.

No guide can cover all situations that could arise during a notification. This guide is intended to highlight the key duties and responsibilities of the notification team members and ease some of the anxiety often experienced when as individual is called upon to personally notify the deceased or missing member's family. Since no two situations are ever the same, remember that nothing can substitute for common sense, good judgment and sensitivity when making death or serious injury notifications.

Selection of Notification Officers

The Agency Administrator/Line Officer or a person designated by agency leadership is the appropriate individual to make a notification and must be accompanied by at least one other person. Depending upon the situation, a coworker, close friend of the deceased or injured, a chaplain or other member of the clergy, or a law enforcement officer may be appropriate.

Notification should always be made by at least two or even three people and always in person. It is a good idea to consider taking separate cars in case one person needs to pick up a family member who is not home or perhaps accompany a family member to the hospital.

Preparing for the Notification

Key information will need to be gathered prior to making a fatality/serious injury notification, such as:

- The circumstances surrounding the death or injury (be clear what is fact and what is not verified), information on the survivors, medical status if the employee is injured, where the injured/deceased person is right now.

- Verify the address of the next of kin. Decide ahead of arrival who will speak first.

- If notification must be made at the next of kin's workplace, ask for a supervisor and a quiet private room to talk with the next of kin.

- If notification is made at the hospital, the same rules apply. Find a quiet private place for the notification and next of kin's questions and reactions.
- Bring Next of Kin Follow-up Worksheet with you. (See page E-9.)

Determining Primary Next of Kin

Refer to the Emergency Notification Information form that should have been completed by the employee. (See Emergency Notification Information, Appendix A). If not available, determine the primary next of kin. The following order is usually the order to use in notifying the primary next of kin.

- Spouse
- Parents
- Adult children
- Brothers and sisters, to include step-siblings and those acquainted through adoption
- Grandparents
- Persons granted legal custody of the individual by a court decree or statutory provision
- Other relatives in order of relationship to the individual according to civil laws
- If no other persons are available, the county coroner or medical examiner will provide information on who can officially act on the behalf of the deceased.
- The most important issue here is to make absolutely sure that the correct persons are notified.

REMEMBER: Family relationships can be very complicated. Fiancés and significant others, whether or not they live with the injured or deceased person, are not legal next of kin. If you are aware of such an individual, ask the primary next of kin if they want to call/visit the significant other.

Inability to Locate the Primary Next of Kin

If the next of kin is not home, contact neighbors, the police department or local postmaster for information on the next of kin's location (work, out of town, etc.). Take care not to disclose (other than a family-related emergency) the purpose of your contact except to the next of kin. If the next of kin's absence is temporary, you may await their return or go in search of them as appropriate. If the next of kin is out of town and not expected to return shortly, determine their exact location. If it is within reasonable distance, attempt to contact them in person. If not, immediately contact the nearest Agency Administrator to the next of kin's physical location, brief him/her and request notification actions.

Secondary Next of Kin

If primary next of kin is not available, contact the secondary next of kin as identified on the Emergency Notification Information sheet.

First Visit Notification

The first visit will be very difficult and may present new uncomfortable feelings with many varied reactions from each surviving family member/survivor. Remember to be professional, demonstrate empathy and listen carefully. When notifying the next of kin, be yourself. This is not easy; be as natural as possible in speech, manner, and method of delivery. The following are suggested approaches with the family in this first visit:

Identify yourself to the next of kin. Example: "I am [AA title] and this is [name]."
Once you arrive at the residence and have identified yourself, confirm the identity of the next of kin. For example, "Are you Mr. Sam Brown?

As soon as most families of public safety professionals see you, they will know something is wrong. Ask to be admitted into the house, and ask him or her to sit down.

Never make any notification on the doorstop of the house!

Verbally relate to the next of kin in your own words the information that you have. Always use the victim's name.

For example:
"The Chief/Director of the [Agency] has asked me to express his/her regret that your (relationship; husband/wife/son/daughter __[name]___) died/was killed in (city/state) on (date). (State the circumstances). Our deepest sympathy to you and your family in your tragic loss."

Another statement which may be needed is:

"The Chief/Director of the [Agency] has asked me to express his/her regret that your (relationship; husband/wife/son/daughter ___[name]___) has been reported missing/injured in (city/state) since (date). (State the circumstances).

Injury: [Name of victim] is now at (name) hospital/treatment center. If you would like to go there now we can help make arrangements.

Missing: When we receive more information we will let you know immediately. We know this is a very difficult time for you and will try to help in any way we can."

Do not drag on with the process.

Communication

- The persons making the notification should be in professional attire or Agency Class A uniform.

- The first visit should be brief and in private. The main concern is to answer questions and meet the demands and requests from the next of kin. A private meeting will cut down on the confusion that can occur with too many people in the room.

- Confirm the next of kin 's address and obtain telephone numbers for future contact.

- Listen: Your alertness to the needs of the next of kin at this time will help maintain a good rapport with the next of kin. Keep notes for later visits with the next of kin. They will be invaluable when reviewing what was said or done and to ensure all requests and commitments have been fulfilled.

- Offer to call immediate family members, friends or clergy who are available to come and support the family.

- Make sure your first visit is as inconspicuous as possible without calling undue attention to your visit by neighbors.

- Use the word died or killed. Do not down-play with "passed away" or "was lost."

- Inform next of kin that they will be contacted by an agency family liaison within 24 hours to assist them with benefits paperwork and other arrangements.

- Verify that all children have been correctly identified.

- Leave names and phone numbers for the family to reach you, the chaplain or the family liaison. Make sure they can find you.

- Gather information to complete the Next of Kin Follow-up Worksheet. (See page E-9)

<u>Do not promise anything that cannot be delivered</u>.

DON'T in the Notification Process

- Do not notify the primary next of kin by telephone.

- Do not call for a prior appointment to making the initial personal notification.

- Do not hold your notes or a prepared speech in hand when making notification.

- Do not disclose your message to neighbors or other persons to have the next of kin to call you.

- Do not use code words or acronyms which may have been used in the incident.

- Do not hurry words, speak as naturally as possible.

- Do not make statements like, "I know how you feel." or "I know what you're going through."

- Do not physically touch the next of kin in any manner unless there is shock or fainting. Summon medical assistance immediately, if necessary. Limit your discussion to information provided for the notification.

- Do not use your prior experiences or personal conjecture.

- Do not speculate on specific questions relating to the victim's activity when they were killed or injured.

- Most decisions regarding cemetery, funeral director, the type of funeral wanted will not be discussed in the first visit. (The family will need time to think.)

- Never make a promise that is not in your power to keep.

- Do not make a statement or relay information to the next of kin unless you have verified the facts. Relaying false information, conflicting or misleading details regarding the fatality incident can be embarrassing to all parties involved. When you are uncertain about the answer to a question, reply that you do not know but will find out. Collect the facts before you respond and always follow through.

<u>**Do not discuss matters that you are not qualified to discuss.**</u>

<u>**Do not take the victim's personal effects on the first notification.**</u>

Reaction

Upon learning of the death or serious injury of a loved one, individuals may experience symptoms of shock such as tremors and a sudden decrease in blood pressure. Shock is a medical emergency and help should be requested immediately.

The family may want to lash out at the agency or person representing the agency that brings the bad news. Later they may feel that the bearer of bad news did not provide enough assistance or that the person was callous and non-caring. If this problem is encountered, remember it is not personal and it is important to call on the family again.

Before leaving, arrange for a time and location to contact the family the next day. Allow the next of kin time to react and offer your support; and if needed, take them to the hospital, or mortuary. Let them determine if they want to see the deceased.

Grieving family members go through different phases of grief and each react in their own unique way. Some factors that affect stress reactions are the intensity of the event (e.g., violent death vs. heart attack), the next of kin's ability to understand what is happening, and their equilibrium. Below are some examples of reactions:

- Shock, followed closely by denial
- Numbness, inability to follow through or focus
- Panic, emotional release, mostly irrational
- Physical/somatic distress: sleepless, sighing
- Overwhelming loneliness
- Depression
- Guilt, recollection of things done and not done for the deceased
- Hostility/resentment toward the agency, or even God who "allowed" it
- Confusion, brought on by disruption of established routines
- Denial: Next of kin continually denying the death. They might repeat "there must be a mistake."
- Anger: Next of kin lashes out at the notifying official or the agency, the decedent, or themselves
- Negotiation: One normally sees this reaction when a family member is dying. Either the injured person or next of kin negotiates with God for extra time.
- Depression: Next of kin does not care about anything or anybody.
- Acceptance: Next of kin accepts the death and starts to rebuild their lives.

Grief recovery is a long-term process. It takes continued contact and understanding by supporters to get through this period.

Injured Person

One of the first questions the next of kin will ask is where their loved one is located and how do they arrange to see them. It is important to verify the location treating the injured individual or the status of the remains before arriving for the first visit. In cases of serious injury, immediately arrange for transportation of next of kin to the medical facility.

Remains of the Deceased

Often, remains of the deceased are not immediately recoverable or not readily accessible. Be alert to this concern, and answer the questions with care. Also be prepared to answer questions about the possibility of viewing the remains. Remember to use the victim's name.

Normally, remains of the deceased are not available until 24 to 36 hours after an autopsy. This needs to be well communicated to the family. Remains may be delayed for medical reasons, criminal investigations or for proper travel documentation.

The family may want to travel to the site to come home with the remains of the deceased.

Follow-up on the status of the remains and keep the next of kin informed.

Do not wait for the next of kin to ask the status.

Personal Effects

Personal effects should be gathered from the incident site and/or the home unit immediately. Items should not be delivered until later, perhaps days later when the family can deal with it. The items should be delivered in a clean unmarked box. All clothes should be cleaned, made presentable or disposed of at a later date. Anticipate delays due to accident or criminal investigations.

Follow-Up Contact

The Agency Administrator/notifier should make contact as previously agreed upon to check on next of kin's welfare. Key points include the following:

- Expressing concern
- Offering assistance
- Answering questions, particularly unresolved questions from first visit (e.g., visiting the site, travel arrangements to hospital (if a distant location), when remains may be returned)
- Allowing next of kin time to talk
- Follow up on promises and obligations

Staying in touch with next of kin is an important Agency Administrator responsibility. Sometimes this can last years and span multiple Agency Administrators.

Agency Administrator Notification to Coworkers

Take care of family first but do not neglect the notification of coworkers who may have had close relationships with deceased or seriously injured employee(s). The same guidance and sensitivities apply as with notifying the family. It is essential that this be done in person and not by voice mail or e-mail.

- Efforts will be made to notify employees at the current workstation and prior workstation, if applicable.

- Notification of family members must never be delayed pending coworker notification.

- Consideration should be given to temporarily relieving affected coworkers from duty.

- Ensure employees are afforded access to CISM, EAP, or other counseling as appropriate.

- Continue to monitor employees' well being and provide appropriate follow-up.

- Provide opportunity for employees to attend funeral(s)/memorial(s). Many agencies provide administrative leave for this purpose.

Notification for Members of the Public or Contractors

When victim is a member of the public, notification should be made by law enforcement. If the victim is an employee of a contractor, notification should be made directly to the contractor's home office (refer to contract specifications).

Next of Kin Follow-Up Worksheet

This form is to be filled out at the time of notification and retained by the notifier to provide information about the surviving family members and their wishes.

Name of next of kin:

Person providing information (if different):

Address of next of kin:

Community: Zip Code:

Telephone: Home   Work   Cell

Relation to the deceased:

Name of funeral home to which the body of the deceased should be sent:

If the next of kin has no preference in funeral homes, would he or she like the medical examiner to choose one? ☐ Yes   ☐ No

Do any next of kin wish to see the body of the person who has died?
☐ Yes ☐ No ☐ Will decide later

Are there any special items that might have been in the possession of the person who died (such as jewelry or a donor card)? (Identify as best possible.)
List:

Others to be contacted by notifier (other kin, unmarried partners, roommates, etc.):

Name: _____   Phone: _____

Name: _____   Phone: _____

Persons contacted by notifier to provide support to the next of kin:

Name: _____   Phone: _____   Date/Time: _____

Name: _____   Phone: _____   Date/Time: _____

Signature of the notifier: _____   Date _____

KEY CONTACTS DURING CRITICAL INCIDENT
Appendix F

Organization	Contact Name	Phone Numbers
Agency Administrator		
Local Unit Administration Officer		
Local Unit Law Enforcement		
Local Unit PAO/PIO		
Family Liaison		
Servicing Personnel Office		
Freedom of Information Act (FOIA) Coordinator		
Fiscal/Budget		
Servicing Agency Legal Counsel (e.g., Regional/Field Solicitor or Office of the General Counsel)		

PREPARING FOR SERIOUS ACCIDENT INVESTIGATION TEAM:
ACTIONS TO BE TAKEN BY THE LOCAL UNIT
Appendix G

Secure the Site

Upon completion of the rescue and medical assistance, the scene must be secured. This may be done by law enforcement; however it may be done by any responsible person under the direction of the Agency Administrator. The scene must remain secure until released by the accident investigation team. Methods to secure the site:

- Ropes
- Barrier tape
- Cones
- Signs
- Flashing lights
- Posted guards

Do not move equipment, shelters, or any other items at the scene. Do not walk around the scene unless it is necessary for rescue or medical assistance. Nothing should be removed from the scene without permission from the accident investigation team leader or chief investigator. Evidence must be preserved at the scene. Photograph the scene (video or stills) if evidence could be lost before the accident investigation team arrives, such as by rainstorm, washing away ruts or fluid spills.

Autopsies

Request an autopsy for all fatalities. Offer to pay for the autopsy if funding is an issue. Ask your local law enforcement officer or team representative to provide a liaison to the county medical examiner or coroner. Access to emergency (911) logs and police reports may be needed.

In case of a fire-related fatality, immediately provide the county medical examiner or coroner with a copy of the FA 156 *Firefighter Autopsy Protocol* found at:
http://www.usfa.dhs.gov/downloads/pdf/publications/firefighter_autopsy_protocol.pdf

Witness Statements

Identify witnesses for accident investigation team interviews and make sure they stay in the area. If that is not possible and witnesses need to be released, have them write, date and sign a statement before they leave. Use the following procedures.

Separate the witnesses and have them write statements in their own words. Witness statements should be in the witness's own handwriting or typed by them on a computer. The witness statement should include:

- Name, work address, and phone number of the witness
- Time and location of the events
- What attracted the witness's attention to the accident
- Description of the sequence of events leading up to accident
- Environment (weather, lighting, temperature, noise)
- Positions of people, equipment, and material, as well as the witness
- What has been moved, repositioned, turned off or on, or taken from the scene
- What actions the witness took at the accident site
- Other witnesses or involved people (include names if known)

Critical Incident Stress Management

Determine need for, and level of, Critical Incident Stress Management (CISM) and implement accordingly. Advise Serious Accident Investigation Team (SAIT) of CISM actions taken.

Accident Investigation Team Administrative Support

The investigation team will need the following:

- A person to serve as a local unit liaison including phone numbers and fax numbers. (The liaison should not be directly or indirectly involved in the accident).
- Lodging/meeting place for the investigation team (including private interview room). Coordinate with the team leader.
- Office supplies (including flip charts, markers).
- Documentation support (at the discretion of the team leader).
    - Shredder
    - Fax
    - Computers
    - Printer
    - Vehicles
    - Speaker phones
    - Copier

Evidence Collection

Collect all or as much of the following applicable items as possible:

- Radio logs (written and recorded)
- Dispatch logs (occupant emergency plans)
- Maps
- Job Hazard Analyses/Risk Assessment
- Safety briefings
- Team briefings
- Employee training records
- Medical examination records
- Work capacity test results
- Qualifications/certifications (including red cards)
- Work/rest (timesheets) for at least two pay periods (current and before the accident)
- Recent fire assignments
- Equipment maintenance records
- Equipment performance tests
- Inspection documents
- Fire management plan
- RAWS (remote automated weather system information)
- Weather (forecast/conditions)
- Fire behavior
- Incident action plans/personnel lists
- Delegation(s) of Authority
- MOU/agreements
- Specifications/drawings
- Press releases
- Autopsy/toxicology report
- Death certificate
- 911 log
- Witness statements
- Internal policies/guidelines
- Tailgate safety session documentation
- Unit's safety plan

DO NOT collect evidence at the scene unless it is in danger of disappearing. Try to contact the team leader or chief investigator if you think it is necessary to remove evidence from the scene.

Contacts

Designate someone to provide the following:

Family liaison – The purpose of the family liaison is to maintain open lines of communication between the agency and the family. The liaison will provide the family support, assistance, and information during the crisis situation.

Public Affairs Officer (PAO) – If there is significant media interest; contact the agency PAO for assistance.

GLOSSARY
Appendix H

Agency Administrator (AA)
Managing officer of an agency, division thereof, or jurisdiction having statutory responsibility for incident mitigation and management. Examples: NPS Park Superintendent, BIA Agency Superintendent, USFS Forest Supervisor, BLM District Manager, FWS Refuge Manager, State Forest Officer, Fire Chief, Police Chief. *See also:* Line Officer.

Casual Employee or Hire
A person hired and compensated under the Pay Plan for Emergency Workers.

Crisis Communication Coaches
Agency employees who have actual experience dealing with a critical incident and are qualified as incident information officers.

Critical Incident
A fatality or other event that can have serious long-term adverse effects on the agency, its employees and their families, or the community.

Critical Incident Stress Management
An adaptive short-term helping process that focuses solely on an immediate and identifiable problem to enable the individual(s) affected to return to their daily routine(s) more quickly and with a lessened likelihood of experiencing post-traumatic stress disorder.

Defusing
This is an informal session held immediately following the incident, within 24 hours. It is peer support led, and focuses on initial venting of feelings and stress education.

Delegation of Authority
A statement provided to Incident Commander by the agency executive delegating authority and assigning responsibility. The delegation of authority can include objectives, priorities, expectations, constraints and other considerations or guidelines as needed. Many agencies require written delegation of authority to be given to incident commanders prior to their assuming command on larger incidents.

Employee Assistance Program (EAP)
An agency-contracted program that provides employees and their families' access to a variety of counseling and other support services in certain situations.

Entrapment
A situation where personnel are unexpectedly caught in a fire behavior-related, life-threatening position where planned escape routes or safety zones are absent, inadequate, or compromised. An entrapment may or may not include deployment of a fire shelter for its intended purpose. These situations may or may not result in injury. They include "near misses."

Family Liaison The primary contact between the agency and the victim's family.

FTR Fire Time Report (Form OF-288)
The official time reporting form for recording hours worked on an incident.

Incident Command System (ICS)
A standardized on-scene emergency management concept specifically designed to allow its user(s) to adopt an integrated organizational structure equal to the complexity and demands of single or multiple incidents, without being hindered by jurisdictional boundaries.

Incident Management Team (IMT)
The incident commander, and appropriate general and command staff, assigned to an incident.

Line Officer
Managing officer, or designee, of the agency, division thereof, or jurisdiction having statutory responsibility for incident mitigation and management. *See also:* Agency Administrator.

Office of Workers' Compensation Programs (OWCP)
The Federal office, under the Department of Labor, charged with administering the Federal Employees' Compensation Act, which authorizes medical care and compensation for periods of disability for Federal employees who sustain traumatic injuries and occupational diseases in the performance of duty.

Peer Support
Employees or individuals trained in peer counseling CISM process, including CISD and defusings.

Tort
The Agency Federal Tort Claims Act is the avenue a private individual has to file a claim against an employee of the Federal government or the Federal government in general.

ACRONYMS
Appendix I

AD   Administratively Determined

AAR   After Action Review

BIA   Bureau of Indian Affairs

BLM   Bureau of Land Management

BPA   Blanket Purchase Agreement

CISM   Critical Incident Stress Management

DOI   Department of the Interior

EAP   Employee Assistance Program

EFF   Emergency Firefighter

FEMA   Federal Emergency Management Agency

FOIA   Freedom of Information Act

FS   U.S.D.A. Forest Service

FWS   U.S. Fish and Wildlife Service

HRSP   Human Resource Specialist

ICS   Incident Command System

IMT   Incident Management Team

MOA   Memorandum of Agreement

MOU   Memorandum of Understanding

NFFF   National Fallen Firefighters Foundation

NPS   National Park Service

OSHA   Occupational Safety and Health Administration

PIO   Public Information Officer

OWCP   Office of Workers' Compensation Programs

PO   Post Office

SSA   Social Security Administration

USDA   United States Department of Agriculture

USDI   United States Department of the Interior

WFFF   Wildland Firefighter Foundation

SOURCES OF ADDITIONAL INFORMATION
Appendix J

This is a partial list of information and/or sites that may be helpful in your respective situation. You are encouraged to become familiar with these sites, obtain these documents, and any others as needed.

- Interagency Incident Business Management Handbook and Supplements (www.nwcg.gov/pms/pubs/pubs.htm)

- BLM Employee Casualty Guide for Managers and Supervisors (www.blm.gov/nhp/efoia/nhrmc/2000/IB/HRIB2000-108.pdf)

- Local Unit Emergency Operating Plans Wildland Firefighter Foundation (Family Liaison and LODD Tool Kit) (www.wffoundation.org)

- National Fallen Firefighters Foundation (Handling LODD) (www.firehero.org/)

- Department of Justice (Public Safety Officer Benefits Program) (www.ojp.usdoj.gov/BJA/grant/psob/psob_main.html)

- Geographic Area Coordination Centers (www.nifc.gov/nicc/)

- U.S. Fire Administration (www.usfa.dhs.gov)

- International Critical Incident Stress Foundation (www.icisf.org/)

- Interagency Standards for Fire and Fire Aviation Operations (Red Book) (www.nifc.gov/policies/red_book.htm)

- Accident Investigation Resources (www.nifc.gov/safety/accident_resources.htm)

- NWCG Safety and Health Working Team (www.nwcg.gov/team/shwt/index2.htm)

www.ingramcontent.com/pod-product-compliance
Lightning Source LLC
Chambersburg PA
CBHW080907290526
45795CB00007BA/2449